In the Deep, Dark Wood

Paul Humphrey

Illustrated by

Carolyn Scrace

Evans

Look, there's the wood. Are all of the trees the same?

No, some are tall and thin and some are very fat.

Some have dark green leaves.

This wood has got oak trees and birch,
maple, and spruce trees. Let's go into the
wood and explore.

5

Look at all these acorns. What kind of trees will they grow into?

Oak trees

6

That's right. But it takes over a hundred years for one tiny acorn to become an oak tree as big as this one.

7

Look at this seed. It comes from the maple tree.

It looks like a seed with a wing.

That's right. If you throw those seeds in the air they will fly. They have wings so that they fly away from the mother tree. Then they will grow into new trees.

9

Here's a group of spruce trees and look at all the fir cones on the ground. The seeds are hidden right inside.

That's a wood ants' nest. Look closely and you'll see that the whole nest is busy with ants working.

It looks as if the whole surface of the nest is moving!

11

Many different animals and plants make their homes in the wood. Look up there. Can you see the rook building its nest?

What's this funny stuff growing out of this tree stump?

That's called bracket fungus. Fungi are plants that grow on dead wood. Don't touch it. Some fungi are poisonous.

13

Probably a woodpecker, looking for grubs and beetles to eat.

Look at all the white flowers growing
in the wood. They are wood anemones.

Let's turn over the dead log and see
what's underneath.

16

All these creatures are very important.
They eat the dead wood.

17

Look at this muddy place. How do you know animals have been here?

I can see their tracks.

That's right. There are deer tracks, fox tracks and tiny mouse tracks.

And look, here's the mouse peeping out of its hole!

19

Now we're getting near to a clearing. Creep very quietly and see what you can see.

It's a deer and a little fawn.

Their colour helps them to
hide amongst the trees.

They must have heard us and run away. Let's see what else there is in the clearing.

Butterflies and bees. I bet they're visiting the flowers t collect pollen and nectar.

That's right, and look, there is a foxhole.
Do you know what a fox's nest is called?

A den.

Look, something is running along that high branch!

It's a squirrel.

Yes, and it's looking for food. It likes to eat the tender new buds on the trees. If you look high in the trees you might see its nest. It's called a drey.

25

Now here's something interesting. Look at those little balls of bones, feathers and fur on the ground.

What are they?

They are owl pellets. The owl swallows its prey whole. Then it brings up the bones, feathers and fur from its stomach and spits them out in pellets like those.

We saw lots of plants and animals on our walk through the deep, dark wood. How many can you remember? The answers are on the next page, but don't peep until you've tried yourself.

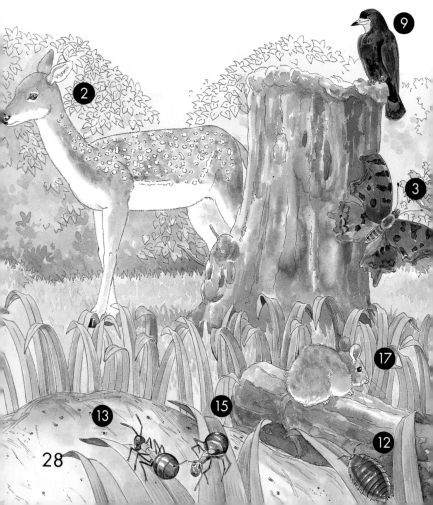

29

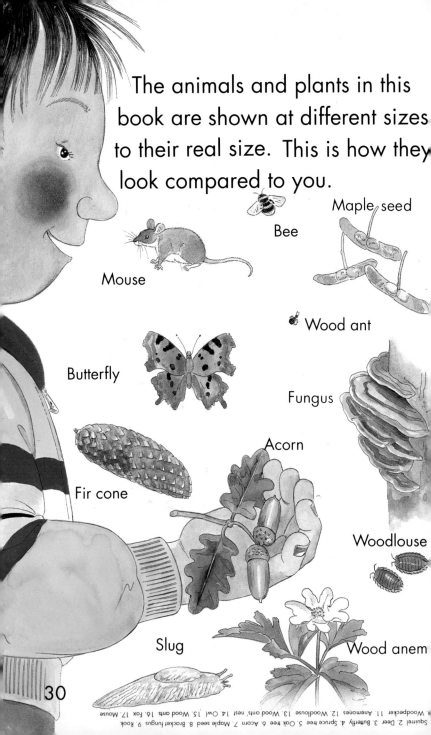

The animals and plants in this book are shown at different sizes to their real size. This is how they look compared to you.

Bee

Maple seed

Mouse

Wood ant

Butterfly

Fungus

Acorn

Fir cone

Woodlouse

Slug

Wood anem

30